core belief™

Bible Study Series
for senior high

WHY
Worship
MATTERS

D1522964

Loveland, Colorado

Why Worship Matters

Core Belief Bible Study Series

Credits

Editors: Siv M. Ricketts and Karl Leuthauser
Creative Development Editors: Ivy Beckwith and Paul Woods
Chief Creative Officer: Joani Schultz
Copy Editor: Pamela Shoup
Art Director: Ray Tollison
Cover Art Director: Jeff A. Storm
Computer Graphic Artist: Eris Klein
Photographer: Craig DeMartino
Production Manager: Gingar Kunkel

ISBN 0-7644-0891-7

10 9 8 7 6 5 4 3 2 1   07 06 05 04 03 02 01 00 99 98

Printed in the United States of America.

core belief

Bible Study Series
for senior high

contents:

the Core Belief: ▼Worship

Worship isn't a foreign concept to young people. They often devote themselves to celebrities of all sorts. Yet celebrities will inevitably disappoint them as they fade away or fall.

But God never fails. He is worthy of our worship. He always does what he says; he never does anything wrong; and when we give him our worship, he draws us closer in a loving embrace.

Through this book, kids can discover that worship is an essential aspect of following God. They'll also explore how worship has both individual and corporate components. Personal worship involves times of expressing praise and gratitude to God, but it should also permeate our lifestyles as we express our praise and serve God through all we do. Corporate worship entails gathering with other believers and together responding to all God is and all he's done.

Worship is a vital element to our Christianity. Not only is God pleased by our worship, he also uses it to refresh us spiritually and renew our lives' focus.

the ▼Helpful Stuff

WORSHIP AS A CORE CHRISTIAN BELIEF
(or Giving Credit Where It's Due)
7

ABOUT CORE BELIEF BIBLE STUDY SERIES
(or How to Move Mountains in One Hour or Less)
10

WHY ACTIVE AND INTERACTIVE LEARNING WORKS WITH TEENAGERS
(or How to Keep Your Kids Awake)
57

YOUR EVALUATION
(or How You Can Edit Our Stuff Without Getting Paid)
63

the ▼Studies

Entering the Worship Zone...   15

THE ISSUE: Worship
THE BIBLE CONNECTION: Psalms 46:10-11; 150; Isaiah 58:6-8; and Romans 12:1
THE POINT: Real worship is a lifestyle.

When God Was Born (on Earth)   27

THE ISSUE: Jesus' Birth
THE BIBLE CONNECTION: Matthew 1:18-25; 2:1-12; 9:1-8; 14:25-36; 21:6-11; 26:6-13; 28:5-10; and Luke 1:46-55; 2:1-20
THE POINT: Jesus inspires us to worship him.

Walking With God   37

THE ISSUE: God's Character
THE BIBLE CONNECTION: Psalm 8; Luke 5:1-11; and Acts 17:24-31
THE POINT: God deserves our worship.

First Things First   47

THE ISSUE: Idolatry
THE BIBLE CONNECTION: Deuteronomy 5:8-10; Matthew 6:19-21, 24; 10:37-39; 16:26
THE POINT: Your priorities reveal what you worship.

▼Worship as a Core Christian Belief

Kids know about worship. They worship musicians, movie stars, professional athletes, and possessions. Kids put posters on their walls, T-shirts on their bodies, headsets over their ears, and even tattoos on their skin—all to exalt human beings and material products.

Unfortunately the "little gods" kids find to praise and honor often disappoint them. The objects of worship become old, out-of-date, or just plain boring.

Thankfully, there's an alternative. God goes beyond fads, marketing, and fame. Worshiping the Creator is exciting, enduring, and fulfilling because God is the only one worthy of our praise and adoration.

This study course will help your kids understand the role that worship plays in their lives. First, they'll focus on ways they can—and do—**worship** throughout their lives every day. They'll discover that God is just as real and available to them at home, in school, or anywhere else as he is when they are in church.

Next, kids will explore how God wanted to be close to us as humans. They will see how the miracle of **Jesus' birth** can inspire us to worship a God who has immense, eternal love for us.

Kids will then explore and discover more about the God they worship. By examining **God's character**, kids will understand that God, in all of his power, glory, and wisdom, deserves our worship.

Finally, kids will think about the things in their lives that they may worship instead of God. **Idolatry** can take many forms, including emulating pop-culture icons and craving material possessions. This study will help kids identify where their priorities lie and examine what they may actually be worshiping in their own lives.

God is worthy of kids' worship. And they need to understand that worship is more than mindlessly singing a couple of hymns or choruses. When kids realize that God wants worship to permeate all we do and they begin to practice true worship, they'll bring honor to God and spiritual enrichment to their lives.

*For a more comprehensive look at this Core Christian Belief, read Group's **Get Real: Making Core Christian Beliefs Relevant to Teenagers.***

DEPTHFINDER
HOW THE BIBLE DESCRIBES WORSHIP

To help you effectively guide your kids toward this Core Christian Belief, use these overviews as a launching point for a more in-depth study of worship.

● **Worship is essential to following God.** The Hebrew word translated "worship" literally means to "bow down." It refers to the honor and reverence shown to a superior being. God is the only one worthy of such worship. In a sense, God both initiates and receives our worship, since the Holy Spirit working in us prompts us to worship God. Through our worship, we express our adoration to God and draw closer to him as we ascribe to him the honor due only to God. We worship God because of who he is, acknowledging his awesomeness and admitting our own smallness.

Worship can be offered through words, music, giving, silent prayers, and many other forms. Worship includes obedience and service; words of praise coming from the mouth of a disobedient Christian mean little to God. We also worship God when we demonstrate a faith commitment through baptism and when we remember Jesus' sacrifice by celebrating the Lord's Supper. (Psalms 24:3-4; 27:8; 29:2; 96:8; Isaiah 6:3; Matthew 4:10; Luke 6:46; John 6:44; Acts 10:46-48; 1 Corinthians 11:23-26; 1 Peter 2:5; Revelation 15:4)

● **Worship should be individual.** Though the Bible describes worship primarily as something the faithful do together, personal worship is an essential part of the Christian's life. The psalmist worshiped God wherever he was, and many times by himself. Worshiping together with other Christians at church does not take the place of individual times of prayer and praise alone. Personal worship involves times of verbally or silently expressing our praise and gratitude to God. But worship is also a lifestyle; part of worshiping God is caring about and helping people who are hurting. (2 Samuel 22:4; Psalms 28:7; 34:1; Isaiah 58:6-11; Micah 6:8; Romans 12:1; Matthew 5:16; 14:22-23)

● **Worship should be corporate.** In both the Old and New Testaments, worship most often appears in the context of God's people gathering together to offer him praise. In worship, the church responds together to who God is and what he has done for us. Corporate worship generally involves active, focused participation by all the members of the local church. Whether people within a congregation are singing, giving offerings, praying, dancing or offering silent or verbal praises, the only people really worshiping are those who genuinely focus on God. When we focus on God in worship, we not only please our Creator, we receive spiritual refreshing and focus in our lives. (Psalms 95:6; 96:1-9; Luke 19:37; 1 Peter 2:9-10; 1 John 1:3)

CORE CHRISTIAN BELIEF OVERVIEW

Here are the twenty-four Core Christian Belief categories that form the backbone of Core Belief Bible Study Series:

The Nature of God	Jesus Christ	The Holy Spirit
Humanity	Evil	Suffering
Creation	The Spiritual Realm	The Bible
Salvation	Spiritual Growth	Personal Character
God's Justice	Sin & Forgiveness	The Last Days
Love	The Church	Worship
Authority	Prayer	Family
Service	Relationships	Sharing Faith

Look for Group's Core Belief Bible Study Series books in these other Core Christian Beliefs!

about

Bible Study Series
for senior high

Think for a moment about your young people. When your students walk out of your youth program after they graduate from junior high or high school, what do you want them to know? What foundation do you want them to have so they can make wise choices?

You probably want them to know the essentials of the Christian faith. You want them to base everything they do on the foundational truths of Christianity. Are you meeting this goal?

If you have any doubt that your kids will walk into adulthood knowing and living by the tenets of the Christian faith, then you've picked up the right book. All the books in Group's Core Belief Bible Study Series encourage young people to discover the essentials of Christianity and to put those essentials into practice. Let us explain...

What Is Group's Core Belief Bible Study Series?

Group's Core Belief Bible Study Series is a biblically in-depth study series for junior high and senior high teenagers. This Bible study series utilizes four defining commitments to create each study. These "plumb lines" provide structure and continuity for every activity, study, project, and discussion. They are:

● **A Commitment to Biblical Depth**—Core Belief Bible Study Series is founded on the belief that kids not only *can* understand the deeper truths of the Bible but also *want* to understand them. Therefore, the activities and studies in this series strive to explain the "why" behind every truth we explore. That way, kids learn principles, not just rules.

● **A Commitment to Relevance**—Most kids aren't interested in abstract theories or doctrines about the universe. They want to know how to live successfully right now, today, in the heat of problems they can't ignore. Because of this, each study connects a real-life need with biblical principles that speak directly to that need. This study series finally bridges the gap between Bible truths and the real-world issues kids face.

● **A Commitment to Variety**—Today's young people have been raised in a sound bite world. They demand variety. For that reason, no two meetings in this study series are shaped exactly the same.

● **A Commitment to Active and Interactive Learning**—Active learning is learning by doing. Interactive learning simply takes active learning a step further by having kids teach each other what they've learned. It's a process that helps kids internalize and remember their discoveries.

For a more detailed description of these concepts, see the section titled "Why Active and Interactive Learning Works With Teenagers" beginning on page 57.

So how can you accomplish all this in a set of four easy-to-lead Bible studies? By weaving together various "power" elements to produce a fun experience that leaves kids challenged and encouraged.

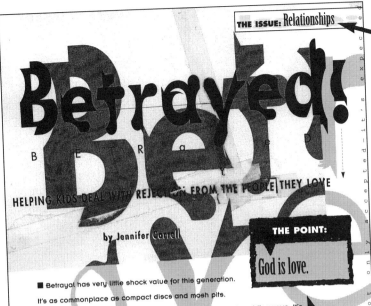

THE ISSUE: Relationships

Betrayed!

HELPING KIDS DEAL WITH REJECTION FROM THE PEOPLE THEY LOVE

by Jennifer Correll

THE POINT:

God is love.

■ Betrayal has very little shock value for this generation. It's as commonplace as compact discs and mosh pits. For many kids today, betrayal characterizes their parents' wedding vows. It's part of their curriculum at school; it defines the headlines and evening news. Betrayal is not only accepted—it's expected. ■ At the heart of such acceptance lies the belief that nothing is absolute. No vow, no law, no promise can be trusted. Relationships are betrayed at the earliest convenience. Repeatedly, kids see that something called "love" lasts just as long as it's convenient... permanence. But deep inside, they hunger to see a

The Study
AT A GLANCE

SECTION	MINUTES	WHAT STUDENTS WILL DO	SUPPLIES
Discussion Starter	up to 5	JUMP-START—Identify some of the most common themes in today's movies.	Newsprint, marker
Investigation of Betrayal	12 to 15	REALITY CHECK—Form groups to compare anonymous, real-life stories of betrayal with experiences in their own lives.	"Profiles of Betrayal" handouts (p. 20), highlighter pens, newsprint, marker, tape
	3 to 5	WHO BETRAYED WHOM?—Guess the identities of the people profiled in the handouts.	Paper, tape, pen
Investigation of True Love	15 to 18	SOURCE WORK—Study and discuss God's definition of perfect love.	Bibles, newsprint, marker
	5 to 7	LOVE MESSAGES—Create unique ways to send a "message of love" to the victims of betrayal they've been studying.	Newsprint, markers, tape
Personal Application	10 to 15	SYMBOLIC LOVE—Give a partner a personal symbol of perfect love.	Paper lunch sack, pens, scissors, paper, catalogs

notes:

● **A Relevant Topic**—More than ever before, kids live in the now. What matters to them and what attracts their hearts is what's happening in their world at this moment. For this reason, every Core Belief Bible Study focuses on a particular hot topic that kids care about.

● **A Core Christian Belief**—Group's Core Belief Bible Study Series organizes the wealth of Christian truth and experience into twenty-four Core Christian Belief categories. These twenty-four headings act as umbrellas for a collection of detailed beliefs that define Christianity and set it apart from the world and every other religion. Each book in this series features one Core Christian Belief with lessons suited for junior high or senior high students.

"But," you ask, "won't my kids be bored talking about all these spiritual beliefs?" No way! As a youth leader, you know the value of using hot topics to connect with young people. Ultimately teenagers talk about issues because they're searching for meaning in their lives. They want to find the one equation that will make sense of all the confusing events happening around them. Each Core Belief Bible Study answers that need by connecting a hot topic with a powerful Christian principle. Kids walk away from the study with something more solid than just the shifting ebb and flow of their own opinions. They walk away with a deeper understanding of their Christian faith.

● **The Point**—This simple statement is designed to be the intersection between the Core Christian Belief and the hot topic. Everything in the study ultimately focuses on The Point so that kids study it and allow it time to sink into their hearts.

● **The Study at a Glance**—A quick look at this chart will tell you what kids will do, how long it will take them to do it, and what supplies you'll need to get it done.

The Bible Connection—This is the power base of each study. Whether it's just one verse or several chapters, The Bible Connection provides the vital link between kids' minds and their hearts. The content of each Core Belief Bible Study reflects the belief that the true power of God—the power to expose, heal, and change kids' lives—is contained in his Word.

THE POINT OF *BETRAYED!*:

God is love.

THE BIBLE CONNECTION

1 JOHN 4:7-21   The Apostle John explains the nature and definition of perfect love.

I n this study, kids will compare the imperfect love defined in real-life stories of betrayal to God's definition of perfect love.

By making this comparison, kids can discover that God is love and therefore incapable of betraying them. Then they'll be able to recognize the incredible opportunity God offers to experience the only relationship worthy of their absolute trust.

Explore the verses in The Bible Connect mation in the Depthfinder boxes throughou understanding of how these Scriptures conn

LEADER TIP for The Study

THE STUDY

DISCUSSION STARTER ▼

Jump-Start (up to 5 minutes) As kids arrive, ask them to thi common themes in movies, books, TV show have kids each contribute ideas for a mas two other kids in the room and sharing their sider providing copies of People maga ine t what's currently showing on television or at their suggestions, write their respo es on n **come up with a lot of great ide s. Even th ent, look through this list an try to disc ments most of these theme have in com**

After kids make several s ggestions, menti responses are connected th the idea of bet
* **Why do you think etrayal is such a**

Betrayed! 17

LEADER TIP for The Study

Because this topic can be so powerful and relevant to kids' lives, your group members may be tempted to get caught up in issues and lose sight of the deeper biblical principle found in The Point. Help your kids grasp The Point by guiding kids to focus on the biblical investigation and discussing how God's truth connects with reality in their lives.

DEPTHFINDER   **UNDERSTANDING INTEGRITY**

Your students may not be entirely familiar with the meaning of integrity, especially as it might apply to God's character in the Trinity. Use these definitions (taken from Webster's II New Riverside Dictionary) and other information to help you guide kids toward a better understanding of how God maintains integrity through the three expressions of the Trinity.

Integrity: 1. Firm adherence to a code or standard of values. 2. The state of being unimpaired. 3. The quality or condition of being undivided.

Synonyms for integrity include probity, completeness, wholeness, soundness, and perfection.

Our word "integrity" comes from the Latin word *integritas*, which means soundness. *Integritas* is also the root of the word "integer," which means "whole or complete," as in a "whole" number.

The Hebrew word that's often translated "integrity" (for example, in Psalm 25:21 [NIV]) is *tam*. It means whole, perfect, sincere, and honest.

CREATIVE GOD-EXPLORATION ▼

Top Hats (18 to 20 minutes) Form three groups, with each trio member from the previous activity going to a different group. Give each group Bibles, paper, and pens, and assign each group a different hat God wears: Father, Son, or Holy Spirit.

Depthfinder Boxes—These informative sidelights located throughout each study add insight into a particular passage, word, historical fact, or Christian doctrine. Depthfinder boxes also provide insight into teen culture, adolescent development, current events, and philosophy.

---

holy Profiles

Your assigned Bible passage describes how a particular person or group responded when confronted with God's holiness. Use the information in your passage to help your group discuss the questions below. Then use your flashlights to teach the other two groups what you discover.

■ Based on your passage, what does holiness look like?

■ What does holiness sound like?

■ When people see God's holiness, how does it affect them?

■ How is this response to God's holiness like humility?

■ Based on your passage, how would you describe humility?

■ Why is humility an appropriate human response to God's holiness?

■ Based on what you see in your passage, do you think you are a humble person? Why or why not?

■ What's one way you could develop humility in your life this week?

Permission to photocopy this handout from Group's Core Belief Bible Study Series granted for local church use.
Copyright © Group Publishing, Inc., Box 481, Loveland, CO 80539.

Leader Tips—These handy information boxes coach you through the study, offering helpful suggestions on everything from altering activities for different-sized groups to streamlining discussions to using effective discipline techniques.

Handouts—Most Core Belief Bible Studies include photocopiable handouts to use with your group. Handouts might take the form of a fun game, a lively discussion starter, or a challenging study page for kids to take home—anything to make your study more meaningful and effective.

The Last Word on Core Belief Bible Studies

Soon after you begin to use Group's Core Belief Bible Study Series, you'll see signs of real growth in your group members. Your kids will gain a deeper understanding of the Bible and of their own Christian faith. They'll see more clearly how a relationship with Jesus affects their daily lives. And they'll grow closer to God.

But that's not all. You'll also see kids grow closer to one another.

That's because this series is founded on the principle that Christian faith grows best in the context of relationship. Each study uses a variety of interactive pairs and small groups and always includes discussion questions that promote deeper relationships. The friendships kids will build through this study series will enable them to grow *together* toward a deeper relationship with God.

ENTERING THE WORSHIP ZONE...

HELPING TEENAGERS LIVE WORSHIPFULLY

by Mike Nappa

■ According to Christian pollster George Barna, there's good news and bad news when it comes to teenage worship attitudes. ■ First, the good news. Half of all American teenagers attend a worship service each week. Two-thirds pray during a normal week. One out of three is involved in a church youth group each week. One of four attends a Bible study each week. And 40 percent of American teenagers attend Sunday school each week. ■ Now the bad news. In spite of this exposure to church worship activities, most American teenagers still lack attitudes toward God that contribute to meaningful worship. In fact, just over half of today's teenagers even agree with the statement that God is "the all-powerful, all-knowing, perfect Creator of the Universe who rules the world today." ■ Says Barna in *Generation Next*, "Fear of God? Frankly, our research suggests that teenagers have a greater fear of walking the streets of their neighborhoods...Stand in awe of the Creator? [Teenagers are] more likely to stand in awe of the natural talents of Michael Jordan." ■ These findings mean it may be tough to teach teenagers about worshiping God. However, God is still God. As our teenagers become more and more intimate with the Almighty Creator, they can't help but worship him. ■ Use this study to expose your teenagers to the intimacy of worshiping God, and to help them better understand the power found in worship as a lifestyle.

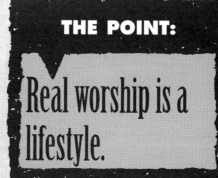

THE POINT:

Real worship is a lifestyle.

The Study
AT A GLANCE

SECTION	MINUTES	WHAT STUDENTS WILL DO	SUPPLIES
Approaching the Worship Zone...	10 to 15	WORSHIPING THE MESSIAH—Tell the story of how George Handel wrote "The Hallelujah Chorus," and listen to the song.	"The Hallelujah Chorus" handouts (pp. 24-25), recording of Handel's "The Hallelujah Chorus," audiocassette or CD player
Entering the Worship Zone...	10 to 15	MINI-MARATHON OF PRAISE—Examine Psalm 150, then spend time praising and adoring God.	Bibles, paper, pencils
	5 to 10	SILENT MESSAGES—Sit or kneel in reverent silence as they meditate on Psalm 46:10-11.	Bibles
	15 to 20	SERVICE WORSHIP—Worship God by serving others, then discuss Isaiah 58:6-8 and Romans 12:1.	Bibles
Being a Worship Zone...	up to 5	POWER OF PRAISE—Spend time singing praise to God.	A praise and worship songbook

notes:

Real worship is a lifestyle.

THE BIBLE CONNECTION

PSALM 46:10-11	The psalmist tells us to be still and know God.
PSALM 150	The psalmist mandates that we praise God in many ways.
ISAIAH 58:6-8; **ROMANS 12:1**	The writers encourage us to worship God through serving others.

I n this study, kids will explore what a lifestyle of worship really means. As part of that exploration, students will experience and discuss the three elements of worship: 1) praise and adoration of God, 2) reverence and respect for God, and 3) service to God and others.

By doing this, kids will gain a new and practical understanding of how to worship God. They'll also be challenged to become people who make worshiping God a part of everyday life.

Explore the verses in The Bible Connection, then examine the information in the Depthfinder boxes throughout the study to gain a deeper understanding of how these Scriptures connect with your young people.

LEADER TIP for The Study

Because this topic can be so powerful and relevant to kids' lives, your group members may be tempted to get caught up in issues and lose sight of the deeper biblical principle found in The Point. Help your kids grasp The Point by guiding kids to focus on the biblical investigation and discussing how God's truth connects with reality in their lives.

THE STUDY

APPROACHING THE WORSHIP ZONE... ▼

Worshiping the Messiah
(10 to 15 minutes)
After everyone has arrived, form four groups (a group can be one person). Give one volunteer in each group a different section of "The Hallelujah Chorus" handout pp. 24-25.

Say: **Let's start off today by learning the story of one of history's most well-known worship songs, "The Hallelujah Chorus." In your groups, listen as someone reads your section of the story, and be prepared to retell that section of the story to someone else. Ready? Go.**

LEADER TIP for Worshiping the Messiah

One excellent contemporary recording of "The Hallelujah Chorus" can be found on the CD, *Handel's Young Messiah*. Published by Word Records, it should be available at your local Christian bookstore.

LEADER TIP for The Study

Whenever groups discuss a list of questions, write the questions on newsprint and tape the newsprint to the wall so groups can answer the questions at their own pace.

Give groups a few minutes to listen to and learn their sections of the story. When kids are ready, have them find partners from each of the other groups to form new groups of four. Be sure each foursome has all parts of the story represented. Then, starting with the person who learned part one of the story, have kids take turns telling their sections of the story to their partners.

While kids are telling each other the story of how Handel wrote "The Hallelujah Chorus," set up an audiocassette or CD player to play a recording of that song.

When everyone has heard the complete story, say: **Now I'd like us to take a few minutes to listen to the worship song Handel said gave him a glimpse of God. As you listen, think about how the song makes you feel about God.**

Play "The Hallelujah Chorus." (If possible, turn it up loud.) Have foursomes discuss these questions:

● **What feelings about God did you have as you listened to "The Hallelujah Chorus"?**

● **Why do you think worshiping God through this song made Handel feel like he was in God's presence?**

Say: **Worship is a powerful and intimate expression of our relationship with God. We need to know, however, that worship is not simply something that happens at church or on a special occasion. Real worship is a lifestyle and involves three things: praise and adoration of God, reverence for God, and service to God. Let's explore what that means.**

ENTERING THE WORSHIP ZONE... ▼

Mini-Marathon of Praise (10 to 15 minutes)

Have kids stay in their foursomes from the previous activity. Distribute paper, pencils, and Bibles to each group.

Say: **In your foursomes, read Psalm 150.** Pause while kids read the Scripture. Then say: **In your groups, write five to ten answers to this question: What does Psalm 150 tell me about worshiping God through praise and adoration?**

After three minutes, have the person in each group wearing the most green report the results of his or her group's discussion. Say: **Now, instead of just talking about worshiping God through praise and adoration, we're going to *do* it!**

Spend several minutes leading kids in a "mini-marathon of praise." You may want to choose three to five of the praise activities that follow, or use some of your own. Here are some "mini-marathon of praise" ideas you might try:

● Sing a familiar praise song.

● Give God a one-minute standing ovation.

● Form a circle and have everyone tell one thing he or she likes about God.

● Have foursomes create imaginary "God Awards" (such as "Best Father of All Time" or "Most Likely to Love"). Then have foursomes "present" their awards to God.

● Lead kids in shouting out the words of Psalm 150.

● Have kids each tell a partner about one time they knew God was active in their lives.

● Have kids imitate musical instruments for one minute to create a "praise orchestra" for God.

● Starting with the letter A and ending with the letter Z, have kids think of words to describe God that begin with each letter of the alphabet.

After the mini-marathon of praise, gather kids in a circle. Have kids volunteer their responses to these questions:

● **What went through your mind during our mini-marathon of praise?**

● **How do you think God felt about our mini-marathon of praise?**

● **Why do you think Psalm 150 tells us to praise God?**

● **What makes it easy or difficult for you to praise God each day?**

● **How might spending time in regular praise and adoration of God affect your daily life?**

Wrap up the activity by saying: **<u>Real worship is a lifestyle</u>, and that includes learning how to praise and adore God on a regular basis.**

"**Be still**, and know that I am God; I will be exalted among the nations, I will be exalted in the earth." **The Lord Almighty is with us;** the God of Jacob is our fortress."

— P S A L M   4 6 : 1 0 - 1 1

LEADER TIP for Silent Messages

For some kids, two minutes of silence may seem like an eternity. For others, three minutes may be only enough time to get them started. You know your group best, so feel free to adjust the time to best fit your group's personality.

Silent Messages (5 to 10 minutes)

Say: **Worship also involves an attitude of reverence and respect for God. Let's take a few moments right now to experience what that can be like.**

Have kids each find a private spot in the room, free from distractions, where they can either sit or kneel. Make sure each person has a Bible open to Psalm 46:10-11.

When everyone is in place, say: **We're going to spend the next three minutes in complete silence. As we experience the silence, read Psalm 46:10-11 several times, and ask God to help you follow the instruction of that Scripture.**

Encourage kids not to be distracted by others during this time of silent reverence. Time three minutes of silence.

After three minutes, have kids find partners to discuss these questions:
● **Describe the feelings you had while we were silent.**
● **What did you discover about worship as you silently read Psalm 46:10-11 and then acted on what you read?**
● **Why do you think it's unusual for us to worship God by simply sitting quietly before him?**
● **What are other ways to show reverence and respect for God?**

Ask pairs to share any insights gained from their discussion. Then say: **Real worship is a lifestyle. Each day we're given the opportunity to worship God through an attitude of reverence for God and respect for others. While we're still in an attitude of quiet reverence, let's take a moment to pray for each other.**

Encourage partners to spend the next minute or so praying for each other, either silently or aloud. Ask kids to pray that their partners experience the peace that comes from reverently and respectfully worshiping God during the coming week.

Service Worship (15 to 20 minutes)

Say: **Real worship is a lifestyle. So far we've learned that worship includes praise to God and reverence for God. A lifestyle of real worship also includes service for God and others. In just a few moments, we're going to leave our classroom and worship God by serving others in our church. But before we go,**

brainstorm with your partner ways you can serve someone and return to our room within five minutes.

Have pairs brainstorm ideas. If kids seem stuck, suggest ideas such as:
● take out the trash,
● clean a bathroom,
● sing a song for an adult class (make sure this is OK with the adults ahead of time),
● wash car windows in the church parking lot,
● pick up trash in the sanctuary (if no one is meeting in there),
● pick up trash around the church grounds,
● clean out drinking fountains,
● create a newsprint "thank you" card for the pastoral staff and hang it in the church lobby,
● write appreciation letters to members of the youth staff, or
● wash chalkboards in empty classrooms.

When kids are ready, have everyone synchronize their watches, then send them out in pairs to perform at least one act of service. Remind kids to be back within five minutes.

After kids return, have pairs join together to form foursomes. Have groups read aloud Isaiah 58:6-8 and Romans 12:1. Have groups discuss these questions:
● **What did your pair do to serve someone?**
● **How was that, in some small way, a fulfillment of what Isaiah 58:6-8 and Romans 12:1 tell us to do?**
● **Why do you suppose God considers service a form of worship?**
● **When is it difficult for you to serve others? Explain.**
● **What's one thing you can do this week to worship God by serving others?**

After discussion, allow time for kids to share any interesting insights they gained. Then say: **Encouraging others is also a way of serving.**

LEADER TIP
for Service Worship

If your group is unable to leave the classroom, have kids look for ways to serve within the room. For example, they could straighten up the classroom, set up chairs for the next class, draw an encouraging mural on the chalkboard, leave a "Well Done!" note for the custodian, and so on.

If your group meets in a home, have kids look for ways to serve each other or the hosts during this activity. For example, kids might straighten the meeting room, wash any dishes used for refreshments, or trade shoulder rubs. Allow kids to go outside if weather permits. They can pull weeds, sweep the walk, or water flowers and trees.

DEPTH FINDER — INDIVIDUAL AND CORPORATE WORSHIP

As we expose our teenagers to worship of God, it's important to also help them understand that worship is both an individual and a corporate experience.

Paul Woods explains individual worship this way: "Personal worship involves times of verbally or silently expressing our praise and gratitude to God. But [personal] worship is also a lifestyle...[of] caring about and helping people who are hurting." (See Psalm 34:1 and Matthew 5:16.)

Lawrence O. Richards expands on Woods' thoughts by saying, "Although worship is a matter of the heart and an expression of one's inner relationship with God, it may also be a public expression of a corporate relationship with God." (See Psalm 95:6-7; Mark 14:26; and Acts 2:46-47.)

Therefore, in our ministry to teenagers, we must remember to encourage kids to worship God both in a corporate setting (for example, at youth group) and also in their own private lives.

(Sources: Real Life Bible Curriculum, Group Publishing, Inc. and Expository Dictionary of Bible Words by Lawrence O. Richards)

So right now, let's take a moment to encourage each other.

Starting with the person in each foursome wearing the most blue, have kids complete this sentence with two encouraging words that describe the person on their left: "(Person's name), God has blessed you with (blank) and (blank) that you can use to worship him." For example, kids might say, "Tony, God has blessed you with a great laugh and a helpful attitude that you can use to worship him."

"Praise the LORD. Praise God in his sanctuary; praise him in his mighty heavens. Praise him for his acts of power; praise him for his surpassing greatness. Praise him with the sounding of the trumpet, praise him with the harp and lyre, praise him with tambourine and dancing, praise him with the strings and flute. Praise him with the clash of cymbals, praise him with resounding cymbals. Let everything that has breath praise the LORD.

Praise the LORD."

— Psalm 150

Power of Praise

(up to 5 minutes)

Gather everyone in a circle. Say: **Worship is a powerful force in our lives, and <u>real worship is a lifestyle.</u> Today we've experienced worship through music, praise, silent meditation, and service. The more you begin to incorporate these and other forms of worship into your daily life, the more worship will become your lifestyle.** Ask kids to share one thing they learned during this lesson and one way they plan to worship God through their lives this week. Give kids a moment to think before asking for their responses.

When kids have shared, say: **Before we go today, let's experience once more what it feels like to be one of God's "worship zones."**

Lead kids in singing several praise and worship songs. Use songs familiar to your kids that also focus on giving praise and adoration to God.

End this lesson with a brief prayer, asking God to make each of your students "a walking worship zone" during the coming week.

DEPTH FINDER
UNDERSTANDING THE BIBLE

"Offer your bodies as living sacrifices, holy and pleasing to God," says Romans 12:1, "this is your spiritual act of worship."

Theologian Craig S. Keener comments on that statement in Romans, "Ancient Judaism and some philosophical schools often used 'sacrifice' figuratively for praise or for a *lifestyle* of worship; hence, it would be hard for Paul's readers to miss his point here." (The IVP Bible Background Commentary: New Testament)

Unfortunately, it's not too hard for teenagers today to miss Paul's point in Romans 12:1. Too often they've been taught that "worship" means simply sitting in church or singing a few songs.

Imagine how their lives would be different if they grasped the fact that worship is a *lifestyle* characterized by service.

LEADER TIP
for Power of Praise

If your group isn't musical, lead students through some of the ideas from the mini-marathon of praise that you didn't use earlier.

LEADER TIP
for Power of Praise

Any of the following praise and worship songs would be an appropriate closing. All can be found in *The Group Songbook*, published by Group Publishing, Inc. They are: "As the Deer"; "Awesome God"; "Father, I Adore You"; "Great Is the Lord"; "How Majestic Is Your Name"; "I Will Celebrate"; "I'm Gonna Sing, Sing, Sing"; "King Jesus Is All"; "Sing Hallelujah to the Lord"; and "Victory Chant" ("Hail, Jesus, You're My King").

The Hallelujah Chorus

Directions: Photocopy and cut apart this handout for use during the "Worshiping the Messiah" activity.

● ● ● ● ● ● ● ● ● ● ● ● ● ● ● ● ●

Part 1:

More than 250 years ago, George Handel was a musical composer living in England. He accepted an assignment to write the music for a new collection titled *Messiah*. A unique aspect of this collection was that all the words were taken directly from Bible passages.

Part 2:

As he began writing the music for *Messiah*, composer George Handel became consumed with his task. He was so caught up in the worshipful activity of creating this masterpiece that he often simply forgot to eat or sleep.

Part 3:

The finale to George Handel's musical was titled, "The Hallelujah Chorus."
Using the words of Scripture, this song is approximately five
minutes of powerful and triumphant praise to Jesus.
This song has become Handel's most
remembered work.

Part 4:

Just after George Handel finished writing
"The Hallelujah Chorus," his servant
came in the room. He found Handel
sitting at a table with tears streaming down his face.
"I did think I did see all Heaven
before me," said Handel,
"and the
great
God
Himself!"

(Source: *George Frideric Handel: His Personality and His Times* by Newman Flower)

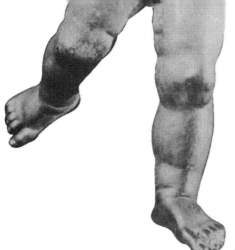

WHEN GOD WAS BORN (on Earth)

A Radical New Look at the Birth of Christ

BY PAMELA T. CAMPBELL

✸ While we probably don't associate diapers, baby bottles, sleepless nights, and talcum powder with royalty, God made no mistake in choosing to bring his Son into this world as a tiny, helpless baby. ✸ Jesus' arrival on earth was just the beginning of many paradoxes: ✸ a baby who is our king, ✸ a king who is our servant, ✸ a servant who is our Prince of Peace, ✸ a Prince of Peace who is a conqueror, and ✸ a conqueror who is the Lamb—the Lamb worthy of our worship. ✸ Most of the people present at Jesus' birth looked beyond their first impressions of baby Jesus' apparent powerlessness to see the significance of his birth for their own lives. This lesson will challenge your students to do the same.

THE POINT:

Jesus inspires us to worship him.

a baby who is our king

The Study
AT A GLANCE

SECTION	MINUTES	WHAT STUDENTS WILL DO	SUPPLIES
Preparing for Jesus' Arrival	up to 5	FAMOUS BIRTHPLACES—Discuss the significance of Jesus' birthplace.	
Responding to Jesus' Arrival	15 to 20	THE INVITATION LIST—Examine how biblical characters invited to meet Jesus responded in worship, and how we respond today.	Bibles, pencils, "Invitations" handouts (p. 35)
	15 to 20	THE INSPIRATION—Examine how Jesus inspired people to worship him, then plan and lead a worship experience.	Bibles
Celebrating Jesus' Arrival	10 to 15	LET US ADORE HIM—Write a Magnificat as a gift of praise.	Bibles, index cards, pencils

notes:

Jesus inspires us to worship him.

THE BIBLE CONNECTION

MATTHEW 1:18-25; 2:1-12	Matthew describes the birth of Jesus and the Magi's visit.
MATTHEW 9:1-8; 14:25-36; 21:6-11; 26:6-13; and 28:5-10	Matthew describes how Jesus inspired people to worship him.
LUKE 1:46-55	Luke recalls Mary's hymn of praise at learning that she'll be the Messiah's mother.
LUKE 2:1-20	Luke describes the birth of Jesus.

I n this study, kids will examine how Jesus inspired biblical characters to worship him. They will reflect on their own response to Jesus and plan and lead worship experiences similar to those described in the Bible. Through this examination, students can deepen their understanding of worship and explore how to worship Jesus on a daily basis.

Explore the verses in The Bible Connection, then examine the information in the Depthfinder boxes throughout the study to gain a deeper understanding of how these Scriptures connect with your young people.

LEADER TIP for The Study

Because this topic can be so powerful and relevant to kids' lives, your group members may be tempted to get caught up in issues and lose sight of the deeper biblical principle found in The Point. Help your kids grasp The Point by guiding kids to focus on the biblical investigation and discussing how God's truth connects with reality in their lives.

THE STUDY

PREPARING FOR JESUS' ARRIVAL ▼

Famous Birthplaces (up to 5 minutes)
Begin this session by saying: **Have any of you ever visited** (insert your birthplace)**? It's quite a city! Many**

LEADER TIP
for The Study

Whenever groups discuss a list of questions, write the questions on newsprint and tape the newsprint to the wall so groups can discuss the questions at their own pace.

DEPTHFINDER — UNDERSTANDING THE BIBLE: GOD AS GIVER

Help your students understand the concept of God as giver by reminding them of James 1:17-18 and John 3:16. Point out that in James 1:17-18, we learn that every good act of giving and every perfect gift comes from the one who created the sun, moon, and stars. Ask your students to consider what "good and perfect" gifts they are thankful for. Then read aloud John 3:16, noting that God's motivation for giving is love and that Jesus is his greatest gift to us. Ask your students to consider how we should respond when receiving such a gift.

people have been born there, including someone whose name you'd recognize. Allow students a few guesses, then reveal that the city is the site of your birth. Ask for a couple of volunteers to briefly share their birthplaces and anything significant about each location.

Say: **When God chose a location for his Son's birthplace, we can assume that he had a reason for choosing as he did.** Discuss the following questions:

● **If you were choosing a place for God to be born, where would you choose?**

● **Why do you think God chose a stable rather than a palace for Jesus' birth?**

● **How has your birthplace affected or defined who you are?**

● **How do you think Jesus' birthplace defined his ministry?**

Say: **Today we're going to discover that <u>Jesus inspires us to worship him</u>. Even Jesus' humble birthplace is an inspiration to worship because it fits well with his desire to reach out to the sick, the lost, and those who wouldn't be permitted in a palace. We can worship God in part because he sent his Son for ordinary people like you and me.**

RESPONDING TO JESUS' ARRIVAL ▼

The Invitation List (15 to 20 minutes) Give each student one character's name and passage from the "Invitation" handout (p. 35).

Then ask kids to form groups with others who share the same character. Tell character groups to read their passages and discuss the following questions:

● **How did your character hear about Jesus' birth?**

● **How did this person respond to the invitation to worship him?**

● **What did this person leave behind to worship Jesus?**

● **How did this person worship Jesus?**

Allow high schoolers about five minutes to work. You can help groups having trouble by using the information found in the Depthfinder, "Responses to Jesus' Birth" (p. 32).

When students have finished answering the questions, ask them to

According to Vine's Expository Dictionary of New Testament Words, worship is not specifically defined in Scripture. However, the five Greek verbs used in the New Testament to express worship are *not* restricted to praise and thanksgiving for God's nature and attributes. In their broadest form, these words indicate that worship includes acts of service motivated by appreciation, awe, devotion, and reverence for God.

form new groups of four with one person from each character group. Tell high schoolers to share what they learned. After a few minutes, ask:

● **What can you learn about worship from the examples of these characters?**

● **In what ways can you respond every day to the news of Jesus' birth?**

Say: **Jesus wants to extend an invitation for you to worship**

"All this took place to fulfill what the Lord had said through the prophet: 'The virgin will be with child and will give birth to a son, and they will call him 'Immanuel' — which means, 'God with us.'"

—Matthew 1:22-23

him. Direct students' attention back to the four questions they discussed in their character groups. Say: **Let's spend a few moments in silence. While it's quiet, answer these questions for yourself. For example, the first question would read, "How did I hear about Jesus' birth?"**

Allow two to three minutes of quiet, then ask kids to offer sentence prayers of thanks for the people who invited them to personally meet Jesus. When students seem to be done praying, close with "amen." Then say: **Celebrating Jesus' birth is more than a once-a-year gift swap and eggnog toast. Because Jesus inspires us to worship him, we can give him gifts of worship every day.**

The Inspiration (15 to 20 minutes)

Ask kids to return to their foursomes, and assign each group one of the following passages from the book of Matthew: 9:1-8; 14:25-36; 21:6-11; 26:6-13; and 28:5-10. Say: **While Jesus was worshiped as a baby, the Gospels also describe people worshiping him at other times during his life. In a moment, you're going to read and discuss a time Jesus inspired someone to worship him. When you've discussed the questions, use the example of worship in the passage to create a short worship experience for our group. For example, if the people in your passage worshiped Jesus through shouting, you could plan to lead us in shouting praises to God.**

DEPTHFINDER RESPONSES TO JESUS' BIRTH

● Joseph (Matthew 1:18-25)—Joseph heard about the conception of Jesus from an angel. He responded in obedience, but we are not told what he felt. He had to leave behind his own ego, his reputation, and his pride as a father to be at the birth of Jesus. Scripture does not reveal how Joseph worshiped Jesus, but we know that he was a person of compassion and that he was obedient, protective, and caring toward the baby.

● Mary (Luke 1:26-38, 46-55)—Mary heard about the conception of Jesus from the angel Gabriel. While she first reacted in fear and wonder, Mary—like Joseph—responded in submissive obedience. She had to set aside her reputation and the normal life of a young woman. Mary gave a hymn of praise, the Magnificat, in response to the news of Jesus' birth.

● Magi (Matthew 2:1-12)—The Magi learned about Jesus' birth from a star in the east. They responded by enduring a long journey to find the baby in hopes of worshiping him. They left behind their studies, homes, and possibly their former religious practices. They worshiped the baby by bowing, showing honor and reverence, and by giving him valuable gifts.

● Shepherds (Luke 2:1-20)—Angels announced the good news of Jesus' birth to the shepherds. They immediately left their flocks and went to Bethlehem. They worshiped the baby by spreading the word of his birth and glorifying and praising God.

Instruct students to discuss these questions:

● **How did Jesus inspire people to worship him?**

● **How did people respond in worship?**

Allow students eight to ten minutes to discuss the questions and plan their worship experiences. Then ask groups to lead the class in the experiences. When all groups have led, ask:

● **Did you feel like <u>Jesus inspired you to worship him</u> through this experience? Why or why not?**

● **What did you learn about Jesus from this experience? about worship?**

● **How does <u>Jesus inspire us to worship him</u> today?**

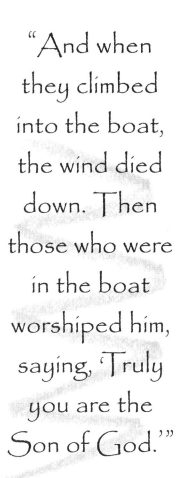

"And when they climbed into the boat, the wind died down. Then those who were in the boat worshiped him, saying, 'Truly you are the Son of God.'"

Matthew 14:32-33

LEADER TIP

for Let Us Adore Him

Before the study, write your own Magnificat as an example. Consider distributing copies so your students have something to refer to as they write.

Let Us Adore Him

(10 to 15 minutes)

Say: **When the angel Gabriel appeared to Mary, she wasn't surprised that the Messiah, the long-awaited Deliverer of the Jews, was coming. She was, however, overwhelmed that she would be his mother. Mary responded to Gabriel's message of God's grace with a hymn of praise called a Magnificat.**

Pass out index cards and pencils to each student. Invite a female to dramatically read aloud Luke 1:46-55, then say: **Mary praised God for the special honor of allowing her to conceive and nurture Jesus. As we close today's lesson, you're going to write your own Magnificat. To get you started, think about these questions:**

● **What great thing has Jesus done for you?**
● **How does** Jesus inspire you to worship him**?**
● **In what way can you worship and rejoice in your Savior?**

When students have finished, ask a few to prayerfully read their Magnificats as gifts of worship.

DEPTH FINDER — A BIRTH PARTY FOR JESUS

As a supplement to this lesson, you could allow students to plan a birth party for Jesus. Students could delegate the responsibilities between four committees: the birth announcement committee, the refreshments committee, the decorations committee, and the creative expression committee. To help your students plan, provide sample birth announcements, menus or cookbooks, decorating ideas, and drama books or songbooks.

High schoolers will want to discuss the advantages and disadvantages of inviting the following groups to the party: your entire church, their friends, or their families. Once a date is set, be sure to check your church calendar for conflicting activities, especially if you're teaching this lesson near Christmas.

Encourage students to be creative in their plans. For example, since the Magi brought gifts to Jesus, the refreshments committee could make food available in wrapped boxes, or the decorations committee might choose decorations in rich, jewel-toned colors to imply royalty.

Joseph
Matthew 1:18-25

Mary
Luke 1:26-38, 46-55

The Magi
Matthew 2:1-12

The Shepherds
Luke 2:1-20

Invitations

Make one copy of this handout for every four students in your group, and cut apart the four sections of each copy.

WALKING WITH GOD

Helping Kids Know God

by Julie Meiklejohn

■ "I am a C. I am a CH. I am a CHRISTIAN." The kids in your youth group may call themselves Christians. They may have heard Bible songs and stories about God since childhood. Others may be just meeting God and the Bible for the first time and learning what it means to be a Christian. But the important question is: Do your students understand what all the stories and teachings have to do with them? ■ This study will introduce your teenagers to God as a real being who desperately wants to have a loving, personal relationship with them. It will help them begin to understand the important difference between *knowing* God rather than just knowing *about* him. This study will help kids see the awesomeness of a God powerful enough to create the whole universe and intimate enough to be their best friend.

THE POINT:

God deserves our worship.

The Study
AT A GLANCE

SECTION	MINUTES	WHAT STUDENTS WILL DO	SUPPLIES
A Call to Worship	5 to 10	INTRODUCING...GOD!—Create introductions for God, and then give thanks for God's presence.	
Proclamation	15 to 20	AN AWESOME GOD!—Examine the story of a biblical character who experiences God's power, and discuss attributes of God that have special meaning to them.	Bibles, newsprint, tape, marker, photocopies of the "Who Is God?" Depthfinder (p. 44), pencils
	10 to 15	MY OWN PERSONAL GOD—Discuss the Apostle Paul's analogies for God, and create their own analogies to describe God.	Bible, paper, pencils, newsprint, marker, tape
An Act of Praise	10 to 15	PRAISE HIS HOLY NAME!—Create artistic expressions of praise in response to Psalm 8.	Bible, paint smocks, canvases, paintbrushes, paints, bowls of water

notes:

God deserves our worship.

THE BIBLE CONNECTION

PSALM 8	The psalmist expresses wonder at the majesty of God's creation.
LUKE 5:1-11	Luke describes Simon Peter's reaction to a miracle performed by Jesus.
ACTS 17:24-31	The Apostle Paul describes God.

I n this study, kids will experience God in a worshipful setting as they explore his character. Through this experience, kids will discover that God deeply desires a close, personal relationship with them.

Explore the verses in The Bible Connection, then study the information in the Depthfinder boxes throughout the study to gain a deeper understanding of how these Scriptures connect with your young people.

LEADER TIP for The Study

Because this topic can be so powerful and relevant to kids' lives, your group members may be tempted to get caught up in issues and lose sight of the deeper biblical principle found in The Point. Help your kids grasp The Point by guiding them to focus on the biblical investigation and by discussing how God's truth connects with reality in their lives.

THE STUDY

A CALL TO WORSHIP ▼

Introducing...God! (5 to 10 minutes) Have kids form pairs, and say: **We have a very special guest here with us today—God! In your pairs, decide how you can best introduce our guest to the group. To get started, think of what you would say if you were introducing a good friend to the group. What would you say about that person? Would you tell about some of the experiences you'd shared? Now apply those ideas to an introduction for God.**

Give pairs a few minutes to work, then have pairs introduce God. Say: **Thank you very much for your fine introductions! We're going to spend some quality time today with God, discovering anew his**

LEADER TIP

for Introducing
...God!

This study contains many different forms of worship, including reflection, prayer, Bible reading and dicussion, personal sharing, active listening, writing, sensory experience, acts of praise, and affirmation. One important element that is not included is music. If your group would enjoy a musical approach to worship, incorporate a few of their favorite praise songs throughout. Possibilities include "Awesome God"; "I'm Gonna Sing, Sing, Sing"; and "I Will Celebrate." These songs can be found in the *Group Songbook*, published by Group Publishing, Inc.

LEADER TIP

for The Study

Whenever you tell groups to discuss a list of questions, write the questions on newsprint and tape the newsprint to the wall so groups can discuss the questions at their own pace.

power and grace and learning of his desire to have an intimate, personal relationship with each one of us. We're going to learn why <u>God deserves our worship</u>. When we worship God, we spend time telling him who he is and how much he means to us. In some ways, it's like encouraging a good friend.

Now I'd like to take a moment for us to thank our guest for being with us today. I'll start in prayer, and then you can share your thanks with God one at a time, silently or aloud. After a few moments, I'll close the prayer. Let's pray. Begin the prayer by thanking God for his presence with your group and asking him to open your hearts and minds as you discover how to truly know and worship him. Allow a few moments for volunteers to pray, and then close by saying "amen."

PROCLAMATION ▼

An Awesome God! (15 to 20 minutes)
Have pairs join with another pair to form groups of four. Make sure groups have Bibles. Say: **Now we're going to hear the story of a man who experienced the power of God in a very real way. One volunteer from each group should read aloud Luke 5:1-11 while the rest of the group follows along. After you've read the passage, discuss the questions on the newsprint. You'll be asked to report your answers in a few minutes.** As kids read, write the following questions on a sheet of newsprint and tape it to the wall.

● **What do you think Simon Peter was feeling?**
● **Why did he respond as he did?**
● **Can you think of a time when you felt like Simon Peter did? Explain.**

DEPTHFINDER   GOD—THREE IN ONE

Prayer is an important part of worship. But what really happens when we pray? In *Mere Christianity*, author C.S. Lewis explores how the triune God acts in and through our prayers:

"An ordinary simple Christian kneels down to say his prayers. He is trying to get in touch with God. But if he is a Christian he knows that what is prompting him to pray is also God: God, so to speak, inside him. But he also knows that all his real knowledge of God comes through Christ, the Man who was God—that Christ is standing beside him, helping him to pray, praying for him. You see what is happening. God is the thing to which he is praying—the goal he is trying to reach. God is also the thing inside him which is pushing him on—the motive power. God is also the road or bridge along which he is being pushed to that goal. So that the whole three-fold life of the three-personal Being is actually going on in that ordinary little bedroom where an ordinary man is saying his prayers. The man is being caught up into the higher kind of life...he is being pulled into God, by God, while still remaining himself."

When groups have discussed the questions, ask volunteers to share their groups' insights. Say: **Simon Peter was awe-struck when he witnessed the power of God. He worshiped God because he experienced God. Though we will never fully understand God, one reason <u>God deserves our worship</u> is because he reveals himself to us through his many attributes, or characteristics.**

Give each person a copy of the "Who Is God?" Depthfinder (p. 44) and a pencil. Say: **Take a few minutes to read through this list of some of God's attributes, and choose one which has special meaning for you. For example, you might choose a characteristic which has been significant in your relationship with God in the past or one that you'd like to know more about. When you've chosen a characteristic, read the Bible verses listed next to it, and think about how that attribute can help you know and worship God more fully. If you'd like, you can jot ideas on the back of your sheet.** Allow kids about five minutes to work and then say: **Share with your group the attribute you chose and explain why.**

When students have shared, ask:

● **After examining some of God's characteristics, why do you think <u>God deserves our worship</u>?**

Say: **Simon Peter fell at Jesus' knees when he saw God's power at work through Jesus. Peter experienced God when he was at work—it had been just an ordinary day for him before meeting Jesus.** Ask:

● **When do you feel closest to God?**

● **How have you seen God in the everyday things in your life?**

Say: **<u>God deserves our worship</u>, and he wants to be in close personal relationship with us all the time, whether we're working, playing, or even sleeping. Even though God is all-powerful, he wants to be the center of our lives.**

"O Lord, our Lord, how majestic is your name in all the earth!"

—Psalm 8:1a

LEADER TIP

for My Own Personal God

You may want to share your own personal analogies of God with your students. Analogies can be specific to your own life, such as "In my life, God is like..."

My Own Personal God (10 to 15 minutes)

Tape a sheet of newsprint to the wall. Have kids form trios with people they didn't work with in the previous activities. Give each trio paper and pencils. Say: **In the book of Acts, the Apostle Paul described God to a group of people who had never experienced God. I'm going to read the passage to you now. While you listen, write down any words or phrases describing God that you hear or that come to mind.**

Slowly read Acts 17:24-31 aloud, pausing to let students write. Then say: **To help his audience begin to understand God, Paul used analogies, or comparisons. He compared God to parts of the common human experience so his listeners could begin to find true knowledge of God.** Ask:

● **What are some of the descriptions of God you wrote down?**

Write kids' answers on the sheet of newsprint.

Say: **In your trios, create a few of your own analogies for God. Think of something you could compare God to that could help you or others understand and know God better. For example, you could say, "God is like a conductor of a mighty orchestra. We each have our important parts to play, but without God's direction, our sound would be just noise. Under God's leadership, together we can create a majestic symphony."**

After trios have created their analogies, ask each trio to share its thoughts with the group. Ask:

"The God who made the world and everything in it is the Lord of heaven and earth and does not live in temples built by hands. And he is not served by human hands, as if he needed anything, because he himself gives all men life and breath and everything else."

—Acts 17:24-25

DEPTH FINDER — A GODLY ANALOGY

Life is often chaotic, and a teenager's life is perhaps especially so. During the craziest times, our teenagers need help putting things into perspective, and of course God is the ultimate Reality. Our awesome Creator God deserves our worship. In *Glimpses of Grace*, author Madeleine L'Engle shares an analogy of God's incredible power at work:

"When I look at the galaxies on a clear night—when I look at the incredible brilliance of creation, and think that this is what God is like, then, instead of feeling intimidated and diminished by it, I am enlarged—I rejoice that I am part of it, I, you, all of us—part of this glory."

● **Do your analogies accurately represent God? Why or why not?**

● **Do you think your analogies and ideas of God will always stay the same? Why or why not?**

● **How can your analogies for God enhance your worship of God?**

● **How can we continue to know God better throughout our lives?**

● **What aspects of God are beyond our understanding?**

Say: **We will never be able to fully know or understand God, but he wants to be a close personal friend to each and every one of us. <u>God deserves our worship</u>, and as we learn and grow, we can discover new ways to be close to him and express our love, devotion, and praise.**

LEADER TIP
for Praise His Holy Name!

If your group meets in the city, high schoolers might be distracted by buildings, traffic, and other man-made sights. Encourage students to move beyond the obvious to what their view says about God. For example, kids might think about how God gave people the ability to create.

AN ACT OF PRAISE ▼

Praise His Holy Name! (10 to 15 minutes)
Set out one canvas and paintbrush for each student. Also set out several colors of paint and bowls of water to clean brushes.

Lead the group outside, and ask each person to find his or her own spot away from the group (but not too far!). Say: **We're going to spend some time worshiping our God. First, listen carefully as I read one of David's songs of praise to God.** Read Psalm 8 aloud to the group, with feeling and expression. Say: **Now, silently look for evidence of God's creation.**

Give students a moment to look around, then ask:

● **How do you feel about God's gift of creation? Explain.**

Say: **God has given us a truly awesome world to live in, and <u>he definitely deserves our worship</u>. Now we're going to create special pieces of artwork as an expression of joy and praise to God for the amazing creation he's given to us.**

Give each person a smock or plastic trash bag to cover his or her

LEADER TIP
for Praise His Holy Name!

Instead of canvas, you can give each student a piece of card stock, construction paper, or even newsprint. If smocks and paints are unavailable, provide students with markers or crayons in a variety of colors and thicknesses. The point is not so much the materials as it is the artistic expression of worship.

Walking With God 43

DEPTHFINDER   WHO IS GOD?

The following chart contains scriptural references and descriptions of God's character.

God Is One	Deuteronomy 6:4; 1 Corinthians 8:4
God Is Truth	Psalm 117:2; Jeremiah 10:10
God Is Infinite	Jeremiah 23:24; Psalm 147:5
God Is All-Knowing	1 John 3:20
God Is Everywhere	Psalm 139:7-12
God Is All-Powerful	Jeremiah 32:17, 27
God Is Unequaled	Isaiah 40:13-25
God Is Perfect	1 Kings 8:27; Psalm 139
God Is a Most Pure Spirit	John 4:24
God Is Invisible	1 Timothy 1:17
God Does Not Have a Human Body	Deuteronomy 4:15-16; John 4:23-24
God Does Not Change	Numbers 23:19; Malachi 3:6; James 1:17
God Is Without Limit	1 Kings 8:27; Jeremiah 23:23-24
God Is Eternal	Psalm 90:2; 1 Timothy 1:17
God Is Incomprehensible	Psalm 145:3; Romans 11:33
God Is the Almighty One	Revelation 1:8; 4:8
God Is Most Wise	Romans 16:27; 1 Corinthians 2:7-11
God Is Most Holy	Isaiah 6:3; Revelation 4:8
God Is Most Free	Psalm 115:3
God Is Most Absolute	Isaiah 44:6; Acts 17:24-25
God Works According to His Will	Romans 8:28; Ephesians 1:11
God Receives Glory	Romans 11:36; Revelation 4:11
God Is Most Loving	1 John 4:8-10
God Is Gracious	Exodus 33:19; 1 Peter 2:2-3
God Is Merciful	Exodus 34:6; James 5:11
God Is Patient	Psalm 86:15; 2 Peter 3:15
God Abounds in Goodness	Psalm 31:19; 52:1; Romans 11:22
God Is Forgiving	Psalm 86:5; Daniel 9:9; Ephesians 1:7
God Rewards Those Who Seek Him	Hebrews 11:6
God Is Just in All His Judgments	Nehemiah 9:32-33
God Hates Sin	Psalm 5:5-6; Habakkuk 1:13
God Is the Creator	Isaiah 40:12, 22, 26
God Is the Shepherd	Genesis 49:24

(Source: Adapted from The Christian Apologetics Notebook by Matthew Slick. Christian Apologetics And Research Ministry Web Page.)

clothes, then say: **I'm going to read the psalm again, one verse at a time. After I read each verse, express your reaction to what the verse says by choosing one color of paint and painting a few brush strokes on a canvas. You can put the paint on the canvas in any fashion you choose—maybe you'd like to paint a wide, sweeping stroke or a fine, gentle line. Don't worry about making it look "perfect." When everyone has painted, I'll move on to the next verse, and you'll move on to the next canvas. Make sure that you paint on a different canvas each time, and remember to rinse your brush before changing colors.**

Read Psalm 8 again, verse by verse, allowing enough time for kids to paint after each verse. After the paintings are finished, have the group step back a bit to admire them. Say: **What a wonderful expression of worship you've created!** Ask:

● **How was this time of worship like or unlike other worship experiences?**

● **What's different about worshiping God by yourself compared to worshiping God with others?**

● **Why do you think God's Word says both are important?**

Have kids form pairs, and say: **Share with your partner ways that each of you helps enhance the other's discovery of the <u>God who deserves our worship</u>. For example, I might say, "Jeff, you help me discover God because you seem to try to find God in everyone."** After pairs have shared, close in prayer, thanking God for being present with the group and for helping kids learn how to truly know and worship him.

LEADER TIP
for Praise His Holy Name!
This activity can be done inside with a few adjustments. Lay newspaper or plastic to protect the floor. To help kids experience God's creation, you may want to bring in plants and play a tape of nature sounds or worship music in the background. You can also have each person examine his or her hands while thinking about the wonder of God's creation.

FIRST THINGS FIRST

GETTING <u>GOD</u> ON TO KIDS' PRIORITY LISTS

by Mikal Keefer

■ It's Monday, and an angel secretary takes notes as God dictates. God begins with cosmic issues, then urgent business, then routine stuff. The angel bows to leave when a scrap of paper flutters out of the Divine Appointment Book and floats to the floor. ■ God notices. "What's that?" he asks. ■ The angel shrugs his shoulders. "That teenager called again. I told the kid you're busy...that you wish you had more time. She said to call when you've got a free minute. She wants to hear from you." ■ God sighs, then wads up the paper and tosses it away. "Well, it's a busy eternal existence. You can't make time for everything." ■ Hardly an accurate picture of how God treats your teenagers—but it may be how your teenagers relate to God. Many teenagers

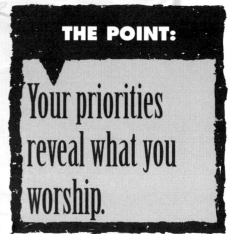

THE POINT:

Your priorities reveal what you worship.

picture God floating somewhere out in orbit—nearby perhaps, but not in need of their attention. Unfortunately, God may be far, *far* from taking first place in their lives. ■ However, God is a jealous God. He wants first place. He *demands* first place. ■ With this study you'll help your kids recognize where God fits into their lives, wrestle with making wise priority choices, and decide if the price of placing God first is worth paying.

The Study
AT A GLANCE

SECTION	MINUTES	WHAT STUDENTS WILL DO	SUPPLIES
Introduction	10 to 15	TIME WARP ARCHAEOLOGY—Decide how their rooms reflect their priorities.	Newsprint, marker, shovel
Bible Exploration	15 to 20	STEPLADDER—Identify, rank, and discuss their priorities.	Bibles, stepladder, index cards, pencils
Life Application	10 to 15	GOD FIRST OR GOD ONLY?—Explore how they can offer their talents and what they value highly to God to use for ministry and worship.	
Closing	10 to 15	JUGGLING PENNY PRAYER—Give to God anything that is interfering with their spiritual growth and discipleship.	Pennies, basket

notes:

THE POINT OF "FIRST THINGS FIRST":

Your priorities reveal what you worship.

THE BIBLE CONNECTION

DEUTERONOMY 5:8-10	God forbids us to make idols.
MATTHEW 6:19-21,24; 16:26	Jesus explains that things on earth don't last.
MATTHEW 10:37-39	Jesus admonishes us to make God our first priority.

I n this study, kids will recognize and evaluate their priorities and compare them with what God says about idolatry.

By doing this, teenagers can commit to placing God first in practical and observable ways and faithfully following God's Word.

Explore the verses in The Bible Connection, then examine the information in the Depthfinder boxes throughout the study to gain a deeper understanding of how these Scriptures connect with your young people.

LEADER TIP
for The Study

Because this topic can be so powerful and relevant to kids' lives, your group members may be tempted to get caught up in issues and lose sight of the deeper biblical principle found in The Point. Help your kids grasp The Point by guiding kids to focus on the biblical investigation and discussing how God's truth connects with reality in their lives.

THE STUDY

INTRODUCTION ▼

Time Warp Archaeology (10 to 15 minutes) When your teenagers arrive, hold up a shovel, trowel, or whisk broom and say: **Welcome to the 45th century! You are archaeologists, and you've just uncovered what appear to be homes from the late 1990's or early 2000's. Your job is to determine what these mysterious people valued most by carefully examining their dwellings. Fortunately, the homes are preserved perfectly. Keep in mind that you know**

LEADER TIP for Time Warp Archaeology

Add dramatic flair to this lesson by decorating your classroom as a classic 45th-century archaeological dig. Wrap the door in tinfoil; place a "Beware Falling Skyscrapers" sign on the door; and give teenagers inexpensive, costume-shop pith helmets to wear.

LEADER TIP for Stepladder

Consider playing soft music while teenagers respond to this activity. *I Believe in Jesus*, an acoustic worship CD from Mercy/Vineyard Publishing, would be an appropriate choice.

LEADER TIP for The Study

Whenever groups discuss a list of questions, write the questions on newsprint and tape the newsprint to the wall so groups can discuss the questions at their own pace.

nothing about the people who once lived in these dwellings; you're drawing conclusions only from what you observe.

Ask your teenagers to form pairs and discuss these questions:

● **In your own dwelling, what appears to be the most important room?**

● **What appears to be the most important piece of furniture?**

● **What appears to be the most precious thing in the dwelling? Explain.**

● **If an archaeologist walked into your room thousands of years from now, what would appear to be most important to you? Why?**

● **If you could tell a future archaeologist what's most important to you, what would you say?**

While pairs report what they concluded from their archaeological studies, list what they say they value most on a piece of newsprint.

Say: **Our values affect what we worship. Worship is simply adoring something and honoring it. For instance, if you have a car and spend enormous amounts of time and effort paying for it, caring for it, and driving it, you may be worshiping the car. Your priorities reveal what you worship.** Ask:

● **Would anything in your room need to change to show future archaeologists that you worship God? If so, what?**

BIBLE EXPLORATION ▼

Stepladder (15 to 20 minutes)

Ask each pair to find another pair and form groups of four. Point to your newsprint list from the "Time Warp Archaeology" activity. Ask:

DEPTHFINDER — THE BOTTOM LINE

Supplement this lesson by taking your teenagers to a nearby cemetery that allows tombstone rubbing (laying thin paper over a tombstone and then rubbing a crayon across the paper to create a "copy" of the tombstone). An older cemetery will have an interesting variety of tombstones.

Your purpose in taking teenagers to the cemetery is to move them out of their comfort zones and bring them to a realization: Their priorities reveal what they worship...and if they worship anything other than God, they'll lose it.

Ask pairs of students to find what they consider to be the saddest tombstone and make a rubbing. Have kids compare notes. Then say: **There are many sad stories in this cemetery, some of which aren't so obvious. Some graves haven't been well-tended. The people in the graves have been forgotten. Some of these large monuments prove that the person who died was wealthy—but where is the money now? When we die—and all of us will—what we've worshiped counts. We can put many things first in our lives, but only Jesus can give us eternal life. Your priorities reveal what you worship—is it Jesus?**

● **What are other things people value highly?**

As kids offer suggestions, add new items to the list, until you have fifteen to twenty. Ask:

● **Are any of these items fundamentally evil?**

● **Are any wrong to value?**

Cross out any items that your kids feel are essentially evil. Say: **The problem comes when we value anything—even something good—more than we value God. When this happens, the person, activity, or thing becomes an idol. Let's take a look at what the Bible says about idols.**

Ask a third of your foursomes to read Deuteronomy 5:8-10; a third to read Matthew 6:19-21, 24 and 16:26; and a third to read Matthew 10:37-39. Direct groups to discuss these questions:

● **What does this passage say about worshiping idols?**

● **What are the consequences of idolatry?**

● **Why do you think God feels so strongly about idols?**

● **How would you sum up this passage in one sentence?**

As kids discuss the questions, set a stepladder in the middle of the room. Ask groups to report their conclusions to the larger group.

Distribute six index cards (or small pieces of paper) and a pencil to each teenager. Say: **Now it's time to vote. Pick six of the things people value from our list on the newsprint, and rank them from one to six, with #1 being the most important, and #6 the least important. List one value on each card. When you've finished, place your #1 value on the top of the ladder, the #2 value on the topmost step, and so on until you've placed the #6 value on the bottom step. You have four minutes.**

LEADER TIP
for Stepladder

Adding a real six- or eight-foot stepladder to your room for this activity will make an impression worth the effort!

If your ladder has more than six steps, adjust the number of values you ask teenagers to select. If you don't have a ladder, take your kids to a stairway so you can make use of the steps. Or draw a ladder on newsprint and use tape to attach index cards.

"No one can serve **two** masters.
Either he will **hate** the one
and **love** the other,

or he will be devoted to the one
and despise the other.
You cannot serve both God and Money."

— **Matthew 6:24**

When students have voted, ask volunteers to gather the cards from each step, and total how many #6, #5, #4, #3, #2, and #1 votes each value receives. Say: **This is probably what we think our values *should* be...but is it how we're living?**

Ask students to spread out a bit and close their eyes. Say: **Imagine Jesus is seated in front of you. What would Jesus say to you about how you use your free time?** Pause while students reflect. Say: **What would Jesus say your priorities are based on how you spend your pocket money?** Pause. **Finally, what would Jesus say about your energy and focus, based on your conversations with your closest friends?**

Ask students to quietly open their eyes and find a partner, then discuss the following questions.

● **Is there a difference between what you say you value most and how you live?**

● **Are there any idols in your life? If so, how do you feel about that?**

● **Would anything need to change in your life to make God your first priority? Explain.**

● **How can you begin to make those changes?**

Lead students in prayer with: **Jesus, we realize <u>our priorities often reveal that we worship other things</u> in your place. Please give us the courage to make the changes needed to put you first in our lives. Amen.**

"**W**hat good will it be for a man if he gains the whole world, yet forfeits his soul? Or what can a man give in exchange for his soul?"

—*Matthew 16:26*

God First or God Only? (10 to 15 minutes)

Ask pairs to form foursomes. Say: **Deciding to put God first comes at a price. In John 17:14-15 Jesus prays: "I have given them your word and the world has hated them, for they are not of the world any more than I am of the world. My prayer is not that you take them out of the world but that you protect them from the evil one."**

Not everyone will applaud if you put Jesus first. Some people will hate you, just like they hated Jesus. You'll make decisions that oppose popular opinion. You'll demonstrate an integrity that bothers some people. You'll act different from some of your friends. You'll make different decisions, and have different priorities, and there'll be no mistaking your identity as a Christian because <u>your priorities will reveal what you worship</u>.

In their groups, ask teenagers to each identify one of their top personal values and to decide how it could be used to honor God. For instance, a talent for basketball could be used to instruct children in the sport and to share faith at the same time.

Ask foursomes to create a pantomime to demonstrate how their values can honor God. While groups take turns presenting their pantomimes, ask viewers to decide what the value is—and how it's being used. Applaud all efforts with enthusiasm! Ask:

● **Does it change your perspective on worship to realize that what you value can be used to worship God? Explain.**

● **How might your life be different if you began looking for ways to worship God through what you value?**

DEPTH FINDER — WHAT IS IDOLATRY?

For the Old Testament Jews, the Ten Commandments outlawed two common forms of idolatry: the worship of any god other than the Lord, and the worship of the Lord in image or form.

In simple terms, an idol is anything that claims the loyalty belonging to God. Though man-made idols are in themselves powerless (contrast to the all-powerful Yahweh), demonic spiritual forces exist, and worshiping idols brings people into contact with them. Deuteronomy 31:16 compares idolatry to spiritual adultery. An idolatrous affair may leave your students spiritually dead.

Idolatry remained a constant struggle for the people of Israel as well as for the early Christians. Even if your students have never seen an intentionally man-made idol, they may be caught up in idolatry by allowing other values to take God's place in their lives. The New Testament associates idolatry with sexual sin and with covetousness (see Galatians 5:19-20 and Ephesians 5:5). Even otherwise good things can become idols, as seen in the examples of the superstitious use of the ephod (Judges 8:27) and the cult of the serpent (2 Kings 18:4).

There is one true God, and he is the Lord. Challenge your students to stay faithful to the one who wants to be their first love.

Juggling Penny Prayer (10 to 15 minutes)

Ask teenagers to form a circle facing in, and give each teenager five pennies. Ask teenagers not to toss pennies at each other or at anything else.

During this activity, you will ask students to juggle pennies, adding one penny at a time, until they're attempting to juggle five at a time. Be sure to pause while reading directions for kids to try juggling an increasing number of pennies.

Ask students to each select their most important penny—the shiniest, oldest, newest, or whatever criteria they choose. Say: **Because our resources of time, energy, focus, and money are limited, we can juggle just so many things. Juggling one thing isn't all that hard.** Ask kids to toss and catch their most important penny. Say: **Juggling two pennies is tougher, because they both take concentration.** Try juggling two pennies, and invite teenagers to try also. When they drop their pennies, encourage kids to pick them up and try again. Instruct students to juggle more pennies every time you mention a number. Say: **Adding a third,** (pause), **fourth,** (pause), **or fifth** (pause) **makes life all but impossible.**

By this point pennies will be flying everywhere. Stop the action and focus kids' attention on yourself. Ask:

● **Were you able to focus your attention on your most important penny while juggling? Why or why not?**

● **How was this activity like what happens in life?**

● **How do you feel when you're not able to focus on what's important to you?**

Say: **It's hard to give our top value the attention it deserves when we're juggling too many values. It gets lost in the activity or dropped altogether.**

Ask kids to collect their pennies, then hold their most important penny in one hand, and the other four pennies in the other hand. Say: **You lead busy lives. You value many things and many people. Your challenge is to keep your relationship with God the most important thing. Remember, your priorities reveal what you worship.**

DEPTHFINDER — TOO BUSY?

Don't believe for an instant your kids are unwilling or unable to sort out what's important and to make time for it. In 1996, 13.3 million teenagers volunteered 2.4 billion hours—1.8 billion with formal organizations (work valued at $7.7 billion). Plus, 5.5 million teenagers work for a paycheck after school or on weekends.

(Source: Rick Lawrence, "Four Big Fat Lies About Kids," GROUP Magazine, May/June 1997)

In a moment, I'll place an offering basket in the center of our circle. If you're willing to make your relationship with God your most important value, it means you've got to give him anything else you value highly. If your job interferes with your relationship with God, you must be willing to surrender it. If a dating relationship interferes with your relationship with God, you've got to be willing to change it. It's up to you to make first things first.

If you're willing to make God first, drop your other pennies in the basket—but hang on to your most important penny. Carry it with you this week as a reminder of your decision. When you drop your pennies in the basket, silently say, "Lord, I give everything to you. You are the most important thing in my life." You don't have to do this—we'll keep our eyes closed until I close in prayer. Only participate if you mean what you're saying.

Ask teenagers to close their eyes and join you for a brief opening prayer, then model the activity for your students. Continue in silent prayer as teenagers decide whether to participate. When everyone who wishes to participate has done so, close with a brief prayer.

why ▼ Active and Interactive Learning works with teenagers

Let's Start With the Big Picture

Think back to a major life lesson you've learned.
Got it? Now answer these questions:
● Did you learn your lesson from something you read?
● Did you learn it from something you heard?
● Did you learn it from something you experienced?
If you're like 99 percent of your peers, you answered "yes" only to the third question—you learned your life lesson from something you experienced.

This simple test illustrates the most convincing reason for using active and interactive learning with young people: People learn best through experience. Or to put it even more simply, people learn by doing.

Learning by doing is what active learning is all about. No more sitting quietly in chairs and listening to a speaker expound theories about God—that's passive learning. Active learning gets kids out of their chairs and into the experience of life. With active learning, kids get to *do* what they're studying. They *feel* the effects of the principles you teach. They *learn* by experiencing truth firsthand.

Active learning works because it recognizes three basic learning needs and uses them in concert to enable young people to make discoveries on their own and to find practical life applications for the truths they believe.

So what are these three basic learning needs?
1. Teenagers need action.
2. Teenagers need to think.
3. Teenagers need to talk.
Read on to find out exactly how these needs will be met by using the active and interactive learning techniques in Group's Core Belief Bible Study Series in your youth group.

1. Teenagers Need Action

Aircraft pilots know well the difference between passive and active learning. Their passive learning comes through listening to flight instructors and reading flight-instruction books. Their active learning comes through actually flying an airplane or flight simulator. Books and lectures may be helpful, but pilots really learn to fly by manipulating a plane's controls themselves.

We can help young people learn in a similar way. Though we may engage students passively in some reading and listening to teachers, their understanding and application of God's Word will really take off through simulated and real-life experiences.

Forms of active learning include simulation games; role-plays; service projects; experiments; research projects; group pantomimes; mock trials; construction projects; purposeful games; field trips; and, of course, the most powerful form of active learning—real-life experiences.

We can more fully explain active learning by exploring four of its characteristics:

● **Active learning is an adventure.** Passive learning is almost always predictable. Students sit passively while the teacher or speaker follows a planned outline or script.

In active learning, kids may learn lessons the teacher never envisioned. Because the leader trusts students to help create the learning experience, learners may venture into unforeseen discoveries. And often the teacher learns as much as the students.

● **Active learning is fun and captivating.** What are we communicating when we say, "OK, the fun's over—time to talk about God"? What's the hidden message? That joy is separate from God? And that learning is separate from joy?

What a shame.

Active learning is not joyless. One seventh-grader we interviewed clearly remembered her best Sunday school lesson: "Jesus was the light, and we went into a dark room and shut off the lights. We had a candle, and we learned that Jesus is the light and the dark can't shut off the light." That's active learning. Deena enjoyed the lesson. She had fun. And she learned.

Active learning intrigues people. Whether they find a foot-washing experience captivating or maybe a bit uncomfortable, they learn. And they learn on a level deeper than any work sheet or teacher's lecture could ever reach.

● **Active learning involves everyone.** Here the difference between passive and active learning becomes abundantly clear. It's like the difference between watching a football game on television and actually playing in the game.

The "trust walk" provides a good example of involving everyone in active learning. Half of the group members put on blindfolds; the other half serve as guides. The "blind" people trust the guides to lead them through the building or outdoors. The guides prevent the blind people from falling down stairs or tripping over rocks. Everyone needs to participate to learn the inherent lessons of trust, faith, doubt, fear, confidence, and servanthood. Passive spectators of this experience would learn little, but participants learn a great deal.

● **Active learning is focused through debriefing.** Activity simply for activity's sake doesn't usually result in good learning. Debriefing—evaluating an experience by discussing it in pairs or small groups—helps focus the experience and draw out its meaning. Debriefing helps sort and order the information students gather during the experience. It helps learners relate the recently experienced activity to their lives.

The process of debriefing is best started immediately after an experience. We use a three-step process in debriefing: reflection, interpretation, and application.

Reflection—This first step asks the students, "How did you feel?" Active-learning experiences typically evoke an emotional reaction, so it's appropriate to begin debriefing at that level.

Some people ask, "What do feelings have to do with education?" Feelings have everything to do with education. Think back again to that time in your life when you learned a big lesson. In all likelihood, strong feelings accompanied that lesson. Our emotions tend to cement things into our memories.

When you're debriefing, use open-ended questions to probe feelings. Avoid questions that can be answered with a "yes" or "no." Let your learners know that there are no wrong answers to these "feeling" questions. Everyone's feelings are valid.

Interpretation—The next step in the debriefing process asks, "What does this mean to you? How is this experience like or unlike some other aspect of your life?" Now you're asking people to identify a message or principle from the experience.

You want your learners to discover the message for themselves. So instead of telling students your answers, take the time to ask questions that encourage self-discovery. Use Scripture and discussion in pairs or small groups to explore how the actions and effects of the activity might translate to their lives.

Alert! Some of your people may interpret wonderful messages that you never intended. That's not failure! That's the Holy Spirit at work. God allows us to catch different glimpses of his kingdom even when we all look through the same glass.

Application—The final debriefing step asks, "What will you do about it?" This step moves learning into action. Your young people have shared a common experience. They've discovered a principle. Now they must create something new with what they've just experienced and interpreted. They must integrate the message into their lives.

The application stage of debriefing calls for a decision. Ask your students how they'll change, how they'll grow, what they'll do as a result of your time together.

2. Teenagers Need to Think

Today's students have been trained not to think. They aren't dumber than previous generations. We've simply conditioned them not to use their heads.

You see, we've trained our kids to respond with the simplistic answers they think the teacher wants to hear. Fill-in-the-blank student workbooks and teachers who ask dead-end questions such as "What's the capital of Delaware?" have produced kids and adults who have learned not to think.

And it doesn't just happen in junior high or high school. Our children are schooled very early not to think. Teachers attempt to help kids read with nonsensical fill-in-the-blank drills, word scrambles, and missing-letter puzzles.

Helping teenagers think requires a paradigm shift in how we teach. We need to plan for and set aside time for higher-order thinking and be willing to reduce our time spent on lower-order parroting. Group's Core Belief Bible Study Series is designed to help you do just that.

Thinking classrooms look quite different from traditional classrooms. In most church environments, the teacher does most of the talking and hopes that knowledge will transmit from his or her brain to the students'. In thinking settings, the teacher coaches students to ponder, wonder, imagine, and problem-solve.

3. Teenagers Need to Talk

Everyone knows that the person who learns the most in any class is the teacher. Explaining a concept to someone else is usually more helpful to the explainer than to the listener. So why not let the students do more teaching? That's one of the chief benefits of letting kids do the talking. This process is called interactive learning.

What is interactive learning? Interactive learning occurs when students discuss and work cooperatively in pairs or small groups.

Interactive learning encourages learners to work together. It honors the fact that students can learn from one another, not just from the teacher. Students work together in pairs or small groups to accomplish shared goals. They build together, discuss together, and present together. They teach each other and learn from one another. Success as a group is celebrated. Positive interdependence promotes individual and group learning.

Interactive learning not only helps people learn but also helps learners feel better about themselves and get along better with others. It accomplishes these things more effectively than the independent or competitive methods.

Here's a selection of interactive learning techniques that are used in Group's Core Belief Bible Study Series. With any of these models, leaders may assign students to specific partners or small groups. This will maximize cooperation and learning by preventing all the "rowdies" from linking up. And it will allow for new friendships to form outside of established cliques.

Following any period of partner or small-group work, the leader may reconvene the entire class for large-group processing. During this time the teacher may ask for reports or discoveries from individuals or teams. This technique builds in accountability for the teacherless pairs and small groups.

Pair-Share—With this technique each student turns to a partner and responds to a question or problem from the teacher or leader. Every learner responds. There are no passive observers. The teacher may then ask people to share their partners' responses.

Study Partners—Most curricula and most teachers call for Scripture passages to be read to the whole class by one person. One reads; the others doze.

Why not relinquish some teacher control and let partners read and react with each other? They'll all be involved—and will learn more.

Learning Groups—Students work together in small groups to create a model, design artwork, or study a passage or story; then they discuss what they learned through the experience. Each person in the learning group may be assigned a specific role. Here are some examples:

Reader

Recorder (makes notes of key thoughts expressed during the reading or discussion)

Checker (makes sure everyone understands and agrees with answers arrived at by the group)

Encourager (urges silent members to share their thoughts)

When everyone has a specific responsibility, knows what it is, and contributes to a small group, much is accomplished and much is learned.

Summary Partners—One student reads a paragraph, then the partner summarizes the paragraph or interprets its meaning. Partners alternate roles with each paragraph.

The paraphrasing technique also works well in discussions. Anyone who wishes to share a thought must first paraphrase what the previous person said. This sharpens listening skills and demonstrates the power of feedback communication.

Jigsaw—Each person in a small group examines a different concept, Scripture, or part of an issue. Then each teaches the others in the group. Thus, all members teach, and all must learn the others' discoveries. This technique is called a jigsaw because individuals are responsible to their group for different pieces of the puzzle.

JIGSAW EXAMPLE

Here's an example of a jigsaw.

Assign four-person teams. Have teammates each number off from one to four. Have all the Ones go to one corner of the room, all the Twos to another corner, and so on.

Tell team members they're responsible for learning information in their numbered corners and then for teaching their team members when they return to their original teams.

Give the following assignments to various groups:

Ones: Read Psalm 22. Discuss and list the prophecies made about Jesus.

Twos: Read Isaiah 52:13–53:12. Discuss and list the prophecies made about Jesus.

Threes: Read Matthew 27:1-32. Discuss and list the things that happened to Jesus.

Fours: Read Matthew 27:33-66. Discuss and list the things that happened to Jesus.

After the corner groups meet and discuss, instruct all learners to return to their original teams and report what they've learned. Then have each team determine which prophecies about Jesus were fulfilled in the passages from Matthew.

Call on various individuals in each team to report one or two prophecies that were fulfilled.

You Can Do It Too!

All this information may sound revolutionary to you, but it's really not. God has been using active and interactive learning to teach his people for generations. Just look at Abraham and Isaac, Jacob and Esau, Moses and the Israelites, Ruth and Boaz. And then there's Jesus, who used active learning all the time!

Group's Core Belief Bible Study Series makes it easy for you to use active and interactive learning with your group. The active and interactive elements are automatically built in! Just follow the outlines, and watch as your kids grow through experience and positive interaction with others.

FOR DEEPER STUDY

For more information on incorporating active and interactive learning into your work with teenagers, check out these resources:

● *Why Nobody Learns Much of Anything at Church: And How to Fix It,* by Thom and Joani Schultz (Group Publishing) and
● *Do It! Active Learning in Youth Ministry,* by Thom and Joani Schultz (Group Publishing).

---

your evaluation of

Bible Study Series
for senior high

why PRAYER matters

Group Publishing, Inc.
Attention: Core Belief Talk-Back
P.O. Box 481
Loveland, CO 80539
Fax: (970) 669-1994

Please help us continue to provide innovative and useful resources for ministry. After you've led the studies in this volume, take a moment to fill out this evaluation; then mail or fax it to us at the address above. Thanks!

● ● ● ● ● ●

1. As a whole, this book has been (circle one)

not very helpful   very helpful
1   2   3   4   5   6   7   8   9   10

2. The best things about this book:

3. How this book could be improved:

4. What I will change because of this book:

5. Would you be interested in field-testing future Core Belief Bible Studies and giving us your feedback? If so, please complete the information below:

Name _____

Street address _____

City _____ State _____Zip _____

Daytime telephone (____) _____ Date _____

THANKS!